Return to Solitude

Return to Solitude
(Haiku and other short poems)

Gopal Lahiri

HAWAKAL PUBLISHERS

Published by: **Hawakal Publishers**, 185, Kali
Temple Road, Nimta, Calcutta 700049, India.

Website: www.hawakal.com
Contact: info@hawakal.com

First edition: November, 2018

Printed and bound at *S. P. Communications,*
Kolkata

Cover image: Canva

Cover design: Bitan Chakraborty

ISBN-13: 978-93-87883-35-2

Price: INR 300/- [USD 11.00]

To my erudite friend
Atreya Sarma Uppaluri

Introduction

Poetry has always been the art of self-expression in wandering souls but inviting the readers to share experience in a few words in poems is also an old art form especially the Japanese one. Let us look into the evaluation of the fixed format short poems.

Of all these Japanese poetic forms, we all know that the Haiku is the best-known and it is actually a short poem of three lines, consisting of seventeen 'syllables'. Although the poem is divided (5-7-5 syllables) it essentially consists of one line during early days.

Senryû is another Japanese form of short poetry similar to haiku in construction: Three lines with 17 or fewer syllables but senryû tend to be about human quirks, while haiku tend to be about nature.

Tankas are 31-syllable poems that have been a popular and oldest form of poetry in Japan for at least 1300 years. Tanka have changed and evolved over the centuries, but the form of five syllabic units containing 31 (5-7-5-7-7) syllables has remained the same. It is also known that topics have expanded from the traditional expressions of passion and heartache, and styles have changed too.

Most haikus, especially those from Japan, depict nature which reflects a special moment, a disposition, an attitude. Every word is important and contributes to what the poet wants to express.

But haiku constantly evolves, both in Japan and from outside Japan, and is now more of a genre, than a fixed form of counting syllables. It regularly shed its skin of fluid syllabic pattern, making it equally fascinating and refreshing in three short lines (tercet). Even the traditional one-line Haiku are also penned in English.

That is why reading a haiku or any other short poems demand the minute attention of the reader. Here every word is sensitive and important to convey the desired meaning as the silence between the lines is fathomless.

Poetry gives many dimensions in our life. In this collection of Haiku and other short poems, what strikes me most is our unbreakable bond with natural world and the end results are penned here in various short forms. Sometimes a few words open up a large space where the human imagination forms and takes flight.

Being an earth-scientist by profession, nature is the home for my psyche. For nature is where we come from and evolved. In these short poems, I return to wilderness, to solitude for the joy of it.

It may be possible that the reader may not sense this, until he/she reads them again and again. I want to take my readers on a wonderful walk where a little rain is a downpour, where silence is a part of our essence, where a solitary mind is a chorus.

Gopal Lahiri
21 September, 2018

rainbow birds
dipping their long legs
skinned alive.

stretching the old truth
evening melts in your coffee
birds' tweet in silence.

the silence of rain,
fills my hands with darkness
records secret songs.

between my fingers and palms
time crumbles along,
just want your eyes and warmth.

in your palm
all your promises
lay like toys.

shadows are all there
summer in your swollen eyes
nights thin to a veil.

the dark night
lip-reads
a human voice.

gone the Simul tree
the fragrance, the medieval sound
missing your verses.

smile is unexplained
each door carries its story
each window its verse.

west wind sweeps across
put out the modest clay lamp
sky filling with chimes.

still searching those ants
never to be cursed again
evils eyes spread out.

tonight the tiny stars
waltz every now and then
the lady rubbing lips.

emerge from hiding
rage of the herons mellows
there is more to life.

outside, the world
floats like sunlit feathers of birds
leaning against the iron grill.

evening stars
ready to ink a beautiful night
sipping secrets.

dark shadows and ghosts
formless night buries our dream
love to burn in (your) flame.

open the window
the pigeons flutter their wings
crooning like film songs.

outside the courtyard
a jasmine tree waiting to
burst into flowers.

a few stars inhale
the fragrance of the dark night
undress for that light.

they laugh
the murmur of the leaves
overlaps their laughter.

I am always last
on the late last list,
receiving your smile
like passing shower.

your eyes return words
silence follows the footsteps
the darkness flowers.

under the rain clouds
she's there, forlorn, unnoticed
go and retrieve her.

walking side by side
the night bathes in silver light
arm in arm they move
arched roof of the trees all round
envelopes two tender souls

wet shiuli flowers
on your tiny petri dish
sharing my puja.

morning rays
probe the wounds of last night
count your first love.

open window
music floats on
the parapet

childhood
hanging from the sky
tender night.

the
red ball
spreading out
now fades and then
a nice glissade over the rift valleys.

stars stroking stars
I wonder if they know how
time breaks on its own.

an evening that has its eyes
there is river in all of us
the twilight varnishes us in ochre.

sky filling with cries
the scarlet birds dip and swing
still dissolving in the air
the mother's swollen eyes.

the leaders are walking
towards us
with bags of promise and poison.

unfamiliar faces speak
searching for the lapis-lazuli
slowly the galaxies feel distant.

the question I ask
why not let me speak in?

the sound is lulling
not knowing the answer,

the evening is somehow numb, bitter

becomes mine.

flying high
the yellow bird takes with her
autumn colour.

morning
leaves are falling
one by one.

twilight
the orange skies
erasing some dark clouds.

you sit calm and quiet
lighting up every moment
freedom stands apart.

we stay united
under the red tinted sky
be not forgotten.

torrential rain
holding tsunami
in my hand.

the river
collects the evening sun
in silence.

echoing
in the mountain wall
your soulful song.

on your writing desk
the diary pages flapping
lies, lies and more lies.

late evening
some mountain shadows
on the wall.

winds come from the sea
love to see your past footprints
here and everywhere.

clouds melt away
the dry river valley
counting rain drops.

a lonely star
disappears
after the rain.

tears soak the grass
cracks on the rocky terrain
cobalt blue sky.

begin to fall
some rose petals
the last hurrah.

a few words
wrapped in a dirty silk cloth
never raise the voice.

crevice and the gap
questions buried, eyebrows raised
glide into history.

red and russet
over tender green
blowing kisses.

before the dark night
carve out a painful story
mists wrap all around.

all night galaxies
unbutton their deep secrets
unsung harmonies.

I hurry back home
all those sweet little flowers
calling all children.

still surviving
on a piece of paper
the economy.

autumn days
stay in the toasty warm
of the green.

in the breath of fire
our protected shadows
recall stormy night.

she returns
from the profound shadows
of the birds.

a need to escape
from everything around me
your door is closing.

stinks, filth and dust bowl
eclipsed by the glory of
an ochre red sun.

alluring sea walk
I rise with the waves
erasing my small lies.

setting sun
thin as a pale wafer
pure blood now.

night groping its way
for all its true elegance
sky a pure darkness.

those yellow pencils
grow old with me
and my words.

strong wind
each window screams
midnight knock out.

night deepens
midsummer alarm
milky way.

cloudy afternoon
pale sun dies on the glass wall
beyond the green park.

the night is alive
it's time to cross-over
the dark known alley.

fairy lights
ghats lit up with lamps
a tiny bird lost its vowel.

the dark stormy cloud
stretching over the plateau
matching mental mist.

time get stuck in reverse
our tears fall in butchers palm
frozen in cold wind.

it's a magical night
in a haze of vapour lamps
ghosts walk in and out.

sea birds roost
on the back waters
hungry moon.

a sense of warmth
your face in paint and pastel
lights up the dark night.

starry laid-back night
empty landscape feels like a
land that time forgot.

in pitch perfect night
your flame burning in my thoughts
miss you so much dear.

crescent moon
words in lips sing silent songs
flicker of a smile.

take her hands in mine
silence is our best witness
life bursting with seeds.

winter rain
weaves the lost skin
a sharp blade.

sitting on the edge
still look for the crescent moon
the mystery lingers.

summer night
shadows smell the memories
spy film fantasy.

over the window
dry leaves fall in a hurry
my winter sets in.

under the drizzle
their breaths touching each other
a light summer rain.

the music on lips
a shallow stream is flowing
let the sunlight in.

the low hill
a panoply of greens
embracing the meadow.

ready to lash out
those birds on the low branches
their harpoon like beaks.

Grandma
making a comeback
in my obsidian mirror.

Ma and Baba never care
to count the pure redness
in love.

www.ingramcontent.com/pod-product-compliance
Lightning Source LLC
Chambersburg PA
CBHW021933170626
46807CB00007B/3084